# Simple Credit Repair

*A step-by-step system to repairing your credit*

# Table of Contents

What's on your credit report?................................................................. 1

Locate the credit report mistakes........................................................... 15

How to clean it up.................................................................................. 24

10 ways to improve your credit score.................................................... 32

It takes time ........................................................................................... 46

Thank you............................................................................................... 51

# What's on your credit report?

Your credit report is an essential part of your day to day life, even if you may not realize it at first. Your credit report is used by credit lenders, home mortgage lenders, insurance companies and even employers when each of them determine if they should, or should not, work with you. Do you know what is on your credit report? If not, there has never been a better time than right now to find out.

WHAT IS IT?

The first question that must be answered is the most important. What is your credit report? A credit report is a collection of information about you. This information is centered around your specific ability and experience with credit use. Credit, a form of money that is given to individuals to spend and repay over time, is given by lenders only if they believe you are a good risk to them. Every lender must define what level of risk is acceptable to them, but they base their decisions on the past usage of credit by you.

Let's explain. Over time, creditors lend to hundreds and thousands of people. They develop specific algorithms that help them define who is a credit risk by looking at the patterns in the way that individuals spend using credit. They determine how much risk they are willing to take to work with people. Risk is a calculated tool for lenders. The more risk you are, the more they can charge in the form of interest rates and fees.

On the other hand, if there is too much risk from an individual, that individual is unlikely to repay their debts and the lender stands to lose money instead of making it.

What does this mean for you, though? As a borrower, you need creditors to see you in the best light possible. The lenders to the credit reporting agencies directly report the decisions you make regarding credit.

- You obtain a credit card. You use it to make a $100 purchase. The credit card company reports this action to the credit bureaus, which keep track of all of your activity.

- You make a payment on time to the lender. The lender lets the credit bureaus know. This looks good to them. Over time, regular payments increase your credit score.

- You make a late payment on the credit card. The lender reports this to the credit bureaus. This looks bad. Just one late payment will remain on your credit report for up to two years, and can drop your credit score.

This record is kept ongoing from the time you first get some form of credit. The more good notches you get from your creditors the better your credit score is. You may be wondering what a credit score is, too.

A credit score is a numerological representation of the credit report. The credit bureaus take all of the information on you and put it into that complex algorithm to get a number that represents your credit usage.

Credit scores can be under 350 up to 800, depending on the credit bureau. The higher the score is, the better. This shows the company that you are a good credit risk.

High credit scores mean:

- More lenders willing to give you credit

- Lower interest rates on new lines of credit

- More ability to borrow at a higher credit limit

- Lower interest rates possible on credit you already have

The key here is taking your credit score, no matter where it is right now, and improving it. You can do this by understanding your credit report thoroughly and by making smart financial decisions going forward.

There is no instant credit eraser or improvement tool that works to move a 350 credit score up to 700. In fact, the credit bureaus will not tell you what percentage of improvement you will have if you make specific credit decisions. The fact is, the mathematical formula they use is highly guarded. Instead, you will need several things to see improvement with your credit:

- Time

- Dedication to good credit usage

- Removal of any inaccurate information on your credit report

Also note that when creditors consider you for a credit card or loan, they most often use just your credit score, with a brief look at your credit report. Therefore, it is very important to do whatever it takes to get this number up.

HOW TO GET YOUR CREDIT REPORT

Let's start with how to get your credit report in the first place.

To obtain your credit report, you have several options. If you have never obtained a credit report in the past, or have not done so in the last 12 months, your first stop should be a visit to each of the three credit reporting companies:

- TransUnion: http://www.transunion.com/

- Equifax: http://www.equifax.com/home/

- Experian: http://www.experian.com/

Visit each company's website. There, you can request a free credit report. Recently, laws in the United States changed to require that each of the credit reporting agencies to provide consumers with one free copy of their credit report each year. The reason for this is that it is an estimate that more than 80 percent of credit reports have errors or missing information on them.

Think about what that means: 80 percent of people may be paying too much in interest, may not qualify for loans they deserve or may even be turned down for a job because they have a poor credit score, through no fault of their own.

Once you get your credit report cleaned up, it is highly recommended that you invest the time in getting a free credit report at least one time per year from each of these companies to ensure that no errors are present. If you would like to avoid paying for additional credit reports, obtain a credit report from one of the credit bureaus every four months. This way, you do not have to pay for the credit report but get the latest information reported there.

There are also a myriad of websites who will also allow you to download your free credit report from their websites, but they ultimately will just be forwarding you to one of the above websites anyway. However, they are worth checking out for the information that you can find on them. Here are a few:

www.annualcreditreport.com
www.freecreditreport.com
www.creditreport.com
www.freecreditreportinstantly.com

The main thing is that you will want to get your free credit report in order to find out where you stand and how far you have to go to repair your credit. Most of the time when you download your credit report, you will be able to view and save it instantly.

ALREADY DONE SO?

Perhaps you have already obtained your credit report in the recent past. To get another one, you may need to pay for it. Most often, copies of your credit report are available for under $20, though it may be slightly more if you would like to see your actual credit score.

You can purchase the credit report from each of the credit bureaus directly. There are other companies selling these, but monitor the security and the overall cost. You may be able to get a credit report for much less, if you go directly to the credit bureau for it.

The first time you obtain your credit report for the goal of cleaning it up, it is important to obtain a copy of the report from each of the three credit bureaus. As mentioned earlier, later on, you may not need to do this since most information will be the same from each of the lenders. Right now, you need to clean up the credit information on all three reports to ensure that your best foot is forward when it comes to credit usage.

WHAT'S ON YOUR REPORT

Once you get to the credit bureaus, you will need to work through the questions they ask. This is important since it is verifying that you are the person you say you are. Once this process is complete, you will be taken to an online version of your credit report. You cannot change information here directly but rather have to go through a specific reporting process.

Before you get excited to see your information, you will want to look for specific information.

- Notice the number of accounts you have: The higher this number is, the more desperate you look to creditors. You do not want a high number.

- Notice any delinquent notices or collection notices on your report. These are one of the most damaging pieces of information listed on the report.

- Locate the credit card accounts listed. You may notice some that are very old, perhaps even your oldest credit cards. If they are good reports, for example, they are not reporting anything is in collections or overdue, leave them there! The longer you have had credit the more experience you have. It is a good thing to have older cards especially with good histories on your account. Do not remove these.

- Locate the inquiries listed. Inquiries are reported whenever someone requests to see your credit report. There are two types. Some come directly from credit card companies and lenders who you have requested credit from. These are the most important to notice since these work against your credit score. If you have too many inquiries listed, this could mean that you are again desperate for credit. It also drops your credit score. The second type is pre-inquiries where lenders are considering offering you a line of credit. Since you have not requested credit from them, these types of inquiries do not count against you.

The credit report contains a wealth of information. Read through it and take notice of the individual accounts. You should notice each account listed, with information including the credit limit, the age of the account, the lender's name and information and a few green (or other colored) boxes. Each month you have the credit account, this box will change in color or mentions. For example, you may notice a streak of green boxes. This means that you have made your payment on time those months, with one box representing one month. These boxes trail back for two years before they disappear.

Take some time to look through the credit report. Most of these reports are very easy to navigate and they only take a few minutes to browse through. Each of the three credit agencies has also provided you with as much information as you need on the credit report. You may also find a section where the bureau is telling you why you have the marks you have or the credit score you have.

They may give you specific information on how to improve the credit score such as:

- Too many delinquent accounts: making payments on time helps to improve your credit score

- There are too many inquiries on your account

- There are too few credit card accounts open

This is specific information directed at you. Definitely use this as a springboard telling you exactly what you need to do to see improvement in your credit score.

ITS ONLY AS GOOD AS

It is important to note that your credit report is only as good as what your creditors have reported. There are going to be errors on your credit report. Some will matter, some may not. The key here is to notice them and to take action to remove them. When you do this, you will find yourself with an improved report and potentially a higher credit score.

Credit accounts are divided into five categories: real estate, installment, revolving, collection and other.

Here is a better description of each category:

1. Real Estate: First and second mortgage loans on your home.

2. Installment: Accounts comprised of fixed terms with regular payments, such as a car loan.

3. Revolving: Accounts with opened terms with varying payments, such as a credit card account.

4. Collection: Accounts seriously past due that have been assigned to an attorney or collection agency.

5. Other: Accounts where the exact category is unknown. This could include 30-day accounts, such as an American Express card.

Your credit report lists a summary of the details and terms for each account. This summary includes information about the account number, condition, balance, type and pay status for each account. The summary for collection records is slightly different.

The following information is for real estate, installment, revolving and other type records:

- Creditor: The official account name. This name may be different than you expect if your account is managed by a larger financial corporation.

- Account Number: This is an identifying number for your account. Typically, this would be a credit card number for a credit card account or a loan identification number for a mortgage. A portion of the number is hidden for security reasons. A partial account number is all that is needed to file a dispute about the record.

- Condition: This is the account's status as open or closed, according to the most recent update from your creditor.

- Balance: The amount you presently owe on the account based on the last reported activity. Very recent activities may not yet have appeared in the bureaus' computer system so this balance may be a few days out-of-date.

- Type: The account's specific type. Some common types are real estate, automobile, educational and credit card accounts.

- Pay Status: The account's payment status, according to the most recent update from your creditor.

For each account, the report also displays an illustrated payment history over the last 24 months. There will be a key at the top of this section describes each payment history symbol and what it indicates for your account. Green boxes marked "OK" show that your payment was made on time.

Most credit reports also give you more in-depth information about specific accounts. This is also an important part of the credit report you'll want to review for accuracy.

The following information may be reported for your account in this section:

- Past Due: The amount of payment overdue as of the most recent reported activity. Very recent payments may take a few days to appear on your credit report.

- High Balance: The most you have ever owed on this account. In the case of a credit card, this is the highest balance you've ever charged. For a mortgage, it is the initial amount of the mortgage.

- Limits: For a credit card or other revolving account, this is the maximum amount you are approved to borrow.

- Terms: This is the number of payments you have scheduled with a creditor. Most commonly this applies to loan accounts. For example, an auto loan may have a repayment plan scheduled over 36 months and a home loan may have a repayment plan scheduled over 360 months.

- Payment: This is the minimum amount you are required to pay each month toward the account.

- Opened: The date the account was opened.

- Reported: The last date when any activity for this account was shown. Activities include payments, credit card billings and changes in your terms. Very recent activity may not yet show on your account, since it takes time for it to appear in the credit reporting agency's system.

- Responsibility: This indicates your responsibility for the account. For example individual, joint or co-signer.

- Late Payments: A summary of your 30, 60 and 90 day late payments over the past 7 years. Please note that the figures in the seven year history include any late payments shown in the two-year history.

- Remarks: Notes about the status or condition of your account.

**FICO scores range between 300 and 850.**

So, here's what those scores mean:

- Over 750 – you have excellent credit and will be able obtain credit easily

- 720 or more – you still have very good credit and will be able to obtain credit easily

- 660 to 720 – this is an acceptable credit. You can still get loans, but you may pay a higher interest rate

- 620 to 660 – creditors are going to be uncertain about lending you money

- Less than 620 – you have poor credit history and will probably not be able to obtain credit on your own

Knowing the above information makes it obvious that if you need or want to get credit for something, the higher your score is, the better your chances are to not only get credit but get it at a handsome interest rate. If you are in the 660 to 620 range, you may still get a loan, but the interest rate is likely to be higher.

That's why it's important to keep your credit good or establish good credit from the get go. That's where you will need to start.

# Locate the credit report mistakes

There are going to be mistakes on your credit report. The number of mistakes is not as important as noticing them. Each of the three credit bureaus legally must take into consideration the information that you provide to them about mistakes. They do not have to make the changes you request unless the credit lender that put the information there is unable to prove that the information is correct.

In the next chapter, we will outline how to get those mistakes off the report. Before that, though, you need to know what types of mistakes to look for and why you need to remove them. Don't skip this step. If you fail to remove all the information that is incorrect on your credit report, you may not be getting it as clean as you could be.

**WHY ARE THERE MISTAKES?**

Although some people may believe that mistakes on credit reports are deliberate actions by lenders, this is far from the truth, in most cases. In fact, mistakes are just that, mistakes made when someone is typing in information. Nearly all transactions that happen on credit accounts happen through automation.

A computer gets your payment information from a teller who has entered it. This information is reported to the computer holding your account information. The information is then filtered one time per month to the credit bureaus, along with thousands of others' information. Perhaps one time during this process is an actual person noticing your information.

A mistake can happen from information being put into the computer system wrong, or information being missed. It could be that the credit card company's machines read your "9" as a "0" and therefore you were not marked as making payment in full for the month. Many potential mistakes can happen.

**Spotting Identity Theft**

Mistakes can be more severe, though. There are plenty of situations where someone has obtained your personal information and is using it to get credit cards, loans or even driver's licenses. This is called a stolen identity. While it may not seem like something that happens often, it actually does. In one report by USA Today, it is an estimate that one in four homes have a victim within it from identity theft.

Identity theft is one of the largest problems with credit bureaus today. There are countless cases of individuals struggling to take back their identity, too. The key here is for you to keep track of what is happening with your credit report so that you can report suspicious information to the proper authorities as soon as it becomes noticed. The sooner you spot the problem, the easier it is to remove it.

If you feel you have been the victim of identity theft, for virtually any reason, you should report this information to your local police. Most larger cities within the United States now have task forces capable of helping individuals with this type of problem specifically. The key is to get help as soon as you notice the problem.

Report the problem if you notice any of the following on your credit report, especially if more than one instance has occurred:

- You notice someone else's address, or an address you have never lived at, especially out of state information

- You have multiple credit accounts or loans that are not yours nor have never been

- You find aliases on your credit report and have any of the above listed problems as well

If you are not sure if you should report the potential identity theft, make your first step working with the credit reporting agency. They can often provide you with the information you need on who obtained the lines of credit.

TYPES OF CREDIT MISTAKES TO FIND

While mistakes do happen, that does not mean that they are irreversible. The following are some of the most common mistakes you will find on your credit report that should be reported to the credit bureau. You should report these to have them removed.

Remember, it only takes a few minutes to scan your credit report, but looking at the details is where you will find most mistakes. Take the time to go through your credit report to ensure that the information being report is accurate, even with their usage of credit that is potentially in your own name.

**Incorrect Account Information**

One of the largest problems that individuals have with their credit report is information on it that is simply not accurate or does not seem to be their own. Depending on how long you have had credit, you may not remember all of the credit lines you have. For example, you may have signed up for a store credit card ten years ago and never used it. As mentioned earlier, older accounts that have no bad information on them (such as late payments, collection activity) should not be removed from your account. This is especially true of open, but not used credit accounts. These establish the length of time you have had credit, which is a good thing for most credit scores.

Look at the accounts closely. Is the following information correct:

- Is the account one that you have opened? If not, and it has a balance, report it to the credit agency. Follow up with the company about the account.

- Is the account listed providing the right balance information? The account may be on a list up to two months behind the current balance since lenders report only one time per month on the account.

- Is the information on the credit limit, credit type, lender, and account holder correct? Your monthly payment may not be accurate, which could stop some lenders from lending to you down the road.

- Is the payment history accurate? Without including the last two months, is the past payment history right? Are the payments listed as late that are not? This should be in the report if so.

- Is there any other information being reported that is inaccurate? This could be collection activity, judgments, information about bankruptcies that is incorrect, or other information. These should be in the report.

**Old Notations on Accounts**

Another potential problem you may notice on your credit report is information that is old. There is a lot of information available about old debts, accounts, and inquiries that are on your credit report. What should be there and when should it just fade into the past?

While many people would say that you should pay all your debts, it is important to note the legalities of paying debt. If you have a debt that goes unpaid for seven years, and the lender has not made any communication with you over that seven year period, you legally are no longer responsible for the debt. In addition to this, debts can remain on your credit report for up to seven years. After that point, it should fall off your report, unless the debt is active, such as a credit card account you are still using.

What is important to know about this is that if there is a debt being reported on your credit report where there has been no activity for a full seven years, it should be removed from the report, especially if it is unpaid debt. If you have a credit card that has a good record of accomplishment, but you have paid it off and no longer use it, this can again serve as a good history for your credit usage and should be in place.

Old marks on your credit report should automatically be removed, but this does not always happen. In the cases where it does not, it is up to you to have it taken off. Here are some notes to keep in mind:

- Old debt unpaid where there is no communication with you should have removal after two years.

- Old credit accounts should disappear after two years, though some with good credit history may remain longer (and that is good!)

- Bankruptcies and judgments passed against you will remain on your credit report for up to ten years. These cannot have removal until after that time.

You have the right to dispute claims that you find that are older than allowed to be. This can be an important tool for improving your credit report, especially if the older accounts have negative marks on them.

**Inquiries**

As mentioned earlier, there is the need to monitor the number of inquiries you have on your credit report. Inquiries are placed on your report whenever someone has requested a copy of your credit report. For example, if you apply for a credit card, the lender will request a copy of your credit score and report from the credit bureau to find out how much of a risk you are. When they do this, after receiving information from you requesting this account, the inquiry is on the credit report.

Too many inquires can downgrade your credit report. For this reason, be selective in applying for any credit or allowing any company to pull a credit report on you. This includes insurance companies and businesses who want you to work for them.

If you spot inquiries you have not approved, you can have them removed from your credit report. It is essential to be sure you have not approved this inquiry, though. To do so, you will need to use the information provided to your advantage. The inquiry will include the name of the company who pulled the report and their contact information. Call them directly and request information about why they have requested a copy of your credit report. They will tell you.

Many times, you will not recognize the actual lender's name on the credit report, but you will be able to remember the transaction after you have called them and asked a question. If, after speaking with the company, you still do not have any memory of this information, the best course of action is to report the inquiry to the credit bureau. They will then force the company to show proof that you requested the inquiry and remove it if it is not possible to verify the information.

Credit inquiries will stay on your credit report for up to two years. Be sure to keep an eye on them over time and to report any mistakes you may have.

INDENTITY MISTAKES

While we mentioned identity theft, there may be other identity problems on your credit report that are not nearly as serious. Here, someone has not actually stolen your identity, but rather the spelled your name wrong, given you someone else's address or otherwise made mistakes with your credit reporting.

Many times, these errors do not matter. If there is a missing letter in your name, it is likely that the mistake has not affected your credit score in any way. Still, you may wish to clean up your credit report and remove this information from it.

In the following chapter, we talk about reporting processes for removing credit related information. The same process is not followed for identity mistakes such as your name, your employer information, your address or other identifiable information. Instead, you will need to call the credit bureau directly to report these problems. Some of this information is unable to be removed from your credit report and the agency will let you know. Other mistakes can receive attention right away.

It may be important to you to update your employer information. This is done over the phone once there is proof of your identity. You may also want to update your address if it is not correct. You may not be able to remove an address you once lived at, though. If you have never lived at the address, definitely report this to the agency.

**TAKE IT STEP BY STEP**

Your credit report is the only piece of information that most lenders receive about you when you apply for a loan through them. It is essential to consider what is on your report and what should not be there. Go through the credit report one line at a time. It is often helpful to print it out and use the paper version to track what you have reported.

The first time you pull your credit report, you are sure to find more than a few mistakes. It may take you some time to locate them all and to get them repaired. Over time, fewer will be reported as you are more conscious of who you are giving your credit information to.

It is essential to go through your report at the very least one time per year to locate any potential problems with it. You should report problems as they happen!

# How to clean it up

Now that you have taken the time to find the mistakes on your credit report, the next step is to get them off there!

The credit bureaus are only collecting information. They never see accounts or payments. They do not work between you and the lender, either. The first course of action for you to take if you notice a problem is to go to that lender and ask questions. This is particularly helpful for recent information or transactions. For example, perhaps you have noticed that a payment did not post or that someone had it listed as late when it was on time.

Your creditor does have the ability to change remarks left on your credit report. They do not always do this instantly, though. It may take until the next reporting that they provide to the credit bureaus. What is important is that you call them and let them know of the mistake. They can then give you instant access to information. Do they have your payment listed as being late? Did they make a mistake in your credit usage? This information should be understood by you prior to filing a claim directly with the credit reporting agencies. That way you know what the facts are and can deal with them appropriately.

Calling your creditor and asking them questions about your credit report is an option to consider. They may or may not be able to clear up the problem, though. You will still need to ensure that the mistakes are removed from your actual credit report, too. Even if they assure you that the mistakes will receive removal in the next 30 to 60 days, follow up and make sure that this happens.

## CONTACTING THE CREDIT BUREAUS

In most situations, you will want to work through the credit bureaus directly to have any errors or mistakes removed from your credit report. You can do this easily right at the company's website.

All credit reporting agencies have the process of removing the credit mistakes online now. It used to be that you needed to call or mail a letter to the credit bureau to get the process going. Now, credit bureaus have made the process quite simple to do. You simply need to sign into the account you have credited when you obtained the copy of your credit report, fill in some basic information and send it off to the lender. Of course, it is a bit more complex than this but the process is not nearly as complicated as you may expect it to be.

**Go To The Right Credit Bureau**

The first step is to go back to the credit bureau's website. You will need to report the error to the individual credit bureau that s reporting the problem. For example, if you find a mistake on your Experian account, you will need to go to Experian to have it removed. At the same time, though, realize that if the mistake has been reported on all three credit reports, you may need to file a claim against each one. This will allow you to get it removed from each of the company's reports.

Most credit bureaus require you to create an account and password when you sign in to view your credit report. This is helpful because it allows you to come back to your report whenever you need to (they are generally available to you for 30 days from the time you have requested them.)

Once there, you will find a link on the home page, usually, that allows you to "dispute" the report or item. This is generally a link that is located on this page, which will take you to a much more in depth form to fill out. You will be fine with the process if you have a printed copy of your credit report on hand to allow you to navigate easily where you need to go.

Sometimes, the companies will allow you to click a link located directly next to the report that's been filed. For example, next to your credit card lender's name and account information, there may be a link to dispute a claim. There will be another link on the next lender's information for the same reason. This is perhaps one of the easiest ways to report an error on your credit report.

Now that you are there, what should you do?

**YOU'VE FOUND THE PROBLEM: NOW WHAT?**

You know the information being reported about you is incorrect. You are probably a bit angry and annoyed that lenders are seeing this information and there is no simple way to remove the information. If anything, the fact that it will take up to two months to have it removed can also be annoying. Still, the process is in place to ensure that the most accurate information is on your credit report.

Once you have found an error, you will need to fill out a form stating so at the credit bureau's website. This part is easy. You likely will need to provide the following information:

- The item you are disputing (your credit card, your mortgage loan, etc)

- The reason for your dispute (it wasn't late, the information is inaccurate or incomplete, etc)

- Any additional information on why this is the case (proof of a canceled check or statements to back up your claim.)

Generally, the information regarding your proof is not collected from you. Rather, the credit bureau will require that the credit card company or lender verify this information. They will need to show proof that the claim they have made to the credit reporting agency is in fact true. In other words, the burden of proof is on the lender, not on you, the borrower.

This is a good thing because it is often more difficult to prove something is true than to have to prove that something is not true. Once you file a claim with the credit-reporting agency, the creditor must show proof that your claim was actually accurate.

Here is a closer look at the process:

1. You pull a copy of your credit report. You find an error on your report.

2. You contact the credit bureau and let them know this is not accurate. For example, it may be an account that is no longer one you have and does not carry a balance though the report says it is.

3. The credit reporting agency will then contact the creditor. They let them know of your dispute with their claim.

4. The creditor must dig through their records and find the information. Generally, this is available on computers and is fairly accurate. There could have been a mistake when the information was reported. Or, there may be inaccurate information in their system. In either case, they need to show that the information is accurate.

5. The creditor has 30 days from the time you have filed the complaint to straighten out the situation. Most lenders want to report accurately.

Then what, you may ask. Once the claim is with the creditor, the credit reporting bureau has to wait to hear back from the lender. Is this information accurate? If so, can they prove it?

If they find that the information is accurate and they have proof that it is, the lender's claim is reported to the credit reporting agency who then leaves the information on your credit report. There can be no further disputes against the information after that decision. If you have overwhelming proof of the situation, contact the credit bureau again requesting help to resolving the problem. Generally, though, a paper trail is the only way to disprove their claim.

If the creditor comes back and says that they cannot prove the claim they have filed against you, for whatever reason, the credit reporting agency will then remove it from your report. This may help to boost your credit score right away, or it may have no effect, depending on the type of report, the length of time since it was reported and other factors. The key here is that it has been removed and you no longer have to live with the mistake.

If the creditor misses the 30 day deadline for coming back to you about the claim, then the credit reporting agency will remove the mark from your credit report as it cannot be proven. As with the opposite scenario, once this decision occurs, it cannot be reversed.

Within that 30 period you will not know what is happening. After the report has been decided on, you will. The credit reporting agency will report the information to you in a letter mailed directly to your home. This information is usually the final answer and is nearly always the most accurate result.

**Making The Most Out Of Claims**

Filing a claim against something that has been reported on your credit report may feel overwhelming, but the process is very straight forward and really only takes a few minutes to get started. It is not the job of the credit reporting agency to verify the claim further than relying on the information that is provided to them. Don't be angry with or treat the credit bureau wrongly as it is likely the item was reported incorrectly to them. Nevertheless, they are working with you to ensure your credit report is the most up to date and accurate as it can be.

Do take the time to be thorough with your claims and be sure to follow up on them. Provide information to the credit bureau about why you feel that the information is incorrect.

"This information is not right." If you type this into the report, chances are good that they will need a bit more information. You may be required to check boxes to explain further the situation.

"This account was closed on May 5th, 2003 after being fully paid off by a check I have the receipt for." This is much more thorough and gives enough information for the creditor to go back and track down the problem. You may be 100 percent right in both cases, but if not enough information is available; it can be difficult to prove.

Be patient, the credit bureaus are not very friendly in terms of providing you with details about the process and where it stands. Therefore, there is no benefit in calling the company repeatedly and requesting more information.

Also, be sure to check your other credit reports for the same or similar mistakes. It is a good sign if the error only appears on one report even though the other two credit bureaus also report on that account. Yet, the same mistake may have been reported to all three. Go through the accounts and follow up!

Finding mistakes on your credit report is vital to improving your credit score and the way that lenders see you. If you do not take the time to do this, you may find your credit report is suffering. Make sure your credit report is accurate by following this process at least one time each year.

# 10 ways to improve your credit score

Your credit report is one of the most important tools you have in the financial world. It defines who you are to lenders of all types. Removing errors from your credit report, or "cleaning it up" is only one part of the process. You need to ensure that you are doing everything possible to keep your credit report in stellar shape so that you also look great in the eyes of a credit card company or home mortgage lender.

Part of this process is to tackle the errors on your credit report. That is the right place to start since this information is hurting you for no reason. As you wait to find out if the errors will be removed by the credit reporting agency, take some time to work through the following steps.

These ten methods to improving your credit score are simple and straightforward, but they also provide you with the resources you need. They may not be easy to do and most of them require time. Nevertheless, making key decisions right now will help you to get back on track and have a high-ranking credit score.

Keep in mind the importance of a quality credit score. With many banks and lenders tightening their lending practices, they simply are not giving out the types of loans you may be used to getting with an average or lower credit score. In fact, if your score is not in the upper 700's, you may be unable to get a home loan without a significant amount down.

The days of having a 400 credit score and getting a great line of credit may not be back anytime soon.

Therefore, take steps right now to improve your credit score so you do not have to hope that you can get that home of your dreams.

## #1: MONITOR YOUR CREDIT REPORT

As we have talked about, knowing what is on your credit report is the key to being successful at managing it. But, just pulling your credit report one time is simply not going to cut it. You need to know what is happening on your credit report regularly.

It is an option to get a copy of your credit report for free only one time per year from each of the three credit bureaus. This means that you can get a copy of your report every four months for free. Most of the time, the information included on one will be the same as all three reports. Nevertheless, there can be differences, which is where you need to be cautious.

If you have found very few mistakes on your credit report up to this point, do not worry about doing anything more than what you are already doing. As long as you are monitoring the report every four months, you should be all right and you should catch errors often enough.

On the other hand, if you have a credit report that has been full of errors, especially those concerning identity theft or larger scale problems with address mistakes and problems with particular creditors, it is best to look for a service to help monitor your credit. These services are available through each of the credit reporting agencies, TransUnion, Equifax and Experian.

There are a variety of types of service and reporting options to consider here. For example, you may choose to have just a copy of your credit report sent to you each month. You may want to watch your credit more closely and want to have a new report more often, such as every few weeks. You may want to know your credit score, too. The more often you need to know your credit report information, the more costly the reporting costs will be. The credit score is usually an additional cost to the credit report.

Reporting services like these can range in cost from $10 a month up to $30 or $40, depending on the type of service you select. Choose what works best for your individual needs. It may not be necessary to have a product that provides you with a large amount of information or frequent reporting, unless you have been having significant problems.

#2: USE CREDIT WISELY

Credit is like a gift. You get it, but only for as long as you take care of it. Stop taking care of the gift, and it will fall to pieces. It is difficult to pick up those pieces and tries to put the puzzle back together than just to maintain the gift in the first place.

Take credit seriously and only use it when you need to use it. For example, it is important to realize that credit that is used during the month should be paid off within the month. That way you do not pay any financing charges and your balance remains low.

It may be important to know what the credit reporting agencies think is important when it comes to credit reports:

- Low balances compared to the amount of available credit

- Payments are made on time

- You do not have too many credit cards

- The amount of total debt you have is not too high, or higher than what is considered appropriate for your income level. This is a debt to income ratio.

It is best to keep the credit you have low in use. Make your payments on time and be sure that you are monitoring your credit limits as often as possible. Paying off the balance on your credit cards on time is quite helpful to maintain a low balance and saving yourself a good deal of money in the process.

Credit is a necessary for purchasing a home and buying a car, most of the time. You will need it throughout your life, which is why you will need to keep your long-term financial goals in mind when using credit for any reason.

## #3: PAY YOUR DEBT DOWN

If you are like most Americans, you have a sizable amount of debt already. How in the world will you be able to get your credit score up if you are struggling with a large pile of debt? The tips provided here should be a great place to start. The key is to work towards your debt step by step until you can pay it down totally. In other words, if you have a lot of debt, just start working towards paying it down now.

There are two main objectives to consider when paying down debt. Choose the method that works best for you.

1. Pay down your debt by making the minimum payments on all of your accounts except for the one with the lowest amount owed. Pay this one with as much as you can until it is paid off. Then, take all the extra you have (including the minimum payment from the first paid off account) and apply it towards the next lowest debt you have. Keep going one by one. The benefit here is that you are paying down your debt quickly: you will see results more often at first, which is great motivation to keep going.

2. Apply the same practice as in the last method, but this time, arrange your debts by the amount of interest that is charged on them, with the highest debt being paid off first. This way, you are able to pay down the type of debt that is costing you the most. Technically, you will pay less on the debt this way, too.

In either of these options, stop using your credit cards regularly. Put them away. Save them for a rainy day. Put away $1000 into a savings account for emergency needs. Use it just for emergencies. This keeps you from applying too much debt to your credit cards. Eventually, you cut your debts considerably.

#4: MONITOR AND LIMIT INQUIRIES

As mentioned earlier, inquiries on your credit report will detract from it. It is inevitable to have some, especially if you are looking for new lines of credit. The key is to keep them as low as possible. On your credit report, there is a separation between the two types of inquiries, those that affect your credit score and those that do not. The goal is to monitor both. If you are prone to accepting credit cards if offers are sent to you, sign up for a do not mail registry. You can opt out of future credit card offers by visiting the website of the Consumer Credit Reporting Industry at OptOutPrescreen.com. You can also locate the Federal Trade Commission for your state and request that these offers stop that way, too.

While you are watching your credit report, keep an eye on the credit inquiries, too. You definitely have to ensure that those that count against you are monitored. Report anything that should not be there. What about the way that you use those credit inquiries? The best way to keep them off your credit report is to ensure that you are not over applying for lines of credit. Here are some tips:

- Choose one or two cards to apply for at any time. Limit the number of applications you file within 3 to 6 month periods.

- When you are shopping for the best insurance or credit card, ask for quotes from the service providers without allowing them to pull a credit report. Let them know the approximate credit score you have. This will allow you to compare several lines of credit or insurance companies without having to subject your credit report to too many inquiries.

- For larger loans, such as a home mortgage loan or car loan, again obtain quotes for loans based on your approximate credit score. This also protects your credit. Many lenders allow you to do this right online. If they do not, look elsewhere for the loan you need.

### #5: DON'T OVER OBTAIN

Many times, it can seem like lenders are willing to give you an unlimited amount of credit. Beware of this. Lenders may see your credit report and believe you are a good risk. They may not realize that three, four or more credit lenders have also noticed this and also have offered you lines of credit. It is easy to get too much credit.

You may be thinking, "is there such a thing as too much credit?" The answer to this is yes! If you have too much credit, lenders will begin to freeze up on you. The problem is the credit to income ratio, or the amount of money you bring in with the amount of potential credit you have available to you. If you have too much credit, the lender may determine that you are too risky to lend more money to, even if you have a lot of open, available credit.

In this situation, you may not have a problem unless you are hoping to get a large loan such as a home loan or a home equity line of credit. In these situations, you may be limited. Obtain only the amount of credit that you need to have. Even if you do get offers from a variety of other lenders over the course of time, you do not have to get them all!

In situations where you receive an offer for a lower interest rate than the rate you are already paying, consider closing the original line of credit prior to accepting the new line of credit. If the account will close after you pay it off completely and it is not one of your oldest credit cards, you may find closing it to be an easy decision.

**#6 DO USE YOUR CREDIT**

You are likely confused. Didn't we just say not to use credit but to pay down your debt? This is true and should be something that you spend a good deal of time doing. If you are carrying debt month to month, it is likely costing you great deal of money. Paying down your debt as much as possible is a must to get your credit score up. The problem you may encounter, though, is that once you have paid off that credit, you have no real credit history for the current period.

So, what do you need to do? Work to pay down your credit. If you are carrying debt month to month, pay it off as quickly as possible. You will definitely want to maintain only lower balances whenever it is possible to do so.

Once you have it paid down to a level you feel comfortable about paying off within a month's time, use your credit again. However, there are some very strict guidelines to remember here:

1. Only make purchases you can pay off within the month. You want to get the bill and pay off the entire balance.

2. Know your grace period, or the amount of time you can borrow money without accruing any finance charges. Most lenders have a 25-day period between months that allows you to use the credit line and pay it off without incurring any finance costs.

3. Use credit only when you need to. Instead of making large purchases using credit, use it for those costs that you are confident you can repay each month. For example, you may want to use a credit card for your gas purchases throughout the money, knowing you will have the funds to repay the debt. This allows you to accumulate no debt month to month.

Credit card debt is not a good thing. Still, in order to have a good credit history, you will need to use credit from time to time. Show that you are a good credit risk by making payments on time each month to pay off the total amount of money you borrowed throughout the month.

# #7: PAY MORE THAN MINIMUM PAYMENTS

One of the mistakes many people make is to make payments on their accounts but only to make minimum payments. The minimum payment on your account is perhaps the worst payment to make besides no payment at all. Even paying a few extra dollars is better. Here is why.

If you pay just the minimum payment on a loan, any loan, it is likely you will pay that debt for years longer than you need to. On a credit card, borrowing just a few thousand dollars may mean only paying $50 a month to repay this debt. But that minimum payment is only a fraction larger than the finance charges for each month. You will remain in the loan ten, twenty or even thirty years depending on the amount of debt it is. For this reason, it is exceptionally important for individuals who are carrying debt month to month to pay off that debt as quickly as possible by paying more than the minimum payment.

Look at it another way. You may not have thought about paying extra per month on your mortgage payment but this too can help you. For example, if you pay a few hundred dollars extra each month on your loan, or you may payments every other week rather than once a month, you could cut five to ten years off the loan's length. This also means a savings of hundreds of thousands of dollars in interest charges. Use a credit card calculator or mortgage calculator to figure out what you are really paying to borrow those funds and to pay it back so slowly!

## #8: BUILD CREDIT WITH SECURED CREDIT CARDS

Perhaps you already have bad credit. Cleaning up your credit card and removing any of the old, outdated information there should help. You may also see an improvement in your credit score if some of the creditors are unable to prove your obligation to pay the loan. Yet, even when you do clean up your credit report, the damage to it over this period of time can be harsh to your credit score. One way to boost it is to obtain new credit and work towards showing that you are a good risk by making payments on time and keeping your balance low.

Like all good catch 22's, though, to build credit means that you would have to have access to it. The good news is that there are options available for doing just that. These are called secured credit cards. Your goal is to find a credit card that's secured that also reports to credit agencies. Many now do this since it is far more attractive to the lender when it does.

A secured credit line is quite different from a standard line of credit. Here, the credit line you are given is based on the amount of cash you have paid towards the card in the form of a deposit. For example, you pay $1000 of a deposit and therefore have a $1000 credit line of credit to use. You'll use it and make payments on it as you do with a standard line of credit. The difference here is that your balance is there for "just in case" situations where you may default on the loan. The lender has protection from this.

At the same time, your good credit habits are also helping you to get a better credit score since the card is reporting each month to the credit agencies.

### #9: KNOW WHEN YOU NEED HELP

There will be times when you just cannot get out of debt on your own. You may find yourself struggling to make enough money to meet just the minimum payments not to mention paying more than you owe. If you are struggling with your debt load, seek help. There are a variety of for profit and not for profit options to help you to get out of debt.

In order for your credit to improve, you need to get out of debt. If you cannot do this on your own, the next best option is to secure help of a professional who can work with you and your lenders to get the debt paid.

One option to consider is debt counseling. These professionals work with your lenders to get a lower monthly payment, to reduce the amount of interest charged to you and sometimes to lower the amount you owe. You'll be on a monthly payment plan requiring you to make a set amount payment each month. That single payment is divided by the counselor and paid to each of your lenders every month. Debt counseling can initially hurt your credit score, but over time, you will be paying down your debt and therefore find your way out of the debt hole. You may see your credit score increase because you are paying off the debt.

Bankruptcy is another option for some, when all hope is lost in making monthly payments. Take it easy, though. Bankruptcy will put a black mark on your credit report for the next ten years! That is a long time to have a hurt credit score with no way to clean it off your report.

**#10: LIVE THE LIFESTYLE YOU CAN AFFORD**

Perhaps the most important bit of help available to you is this simple sentence. You need to live the type of lifestyle that you can actually afford, not one that is reliant on credit cards. The sad fact is that if you take away all of the debt you had, you probably would have more money per month to buy what you want and to live the way you want to. The key is not to have to pay the finance charges that often hurt the average consumer.

Determine what your lifestyle is by using a cash only system for at least one month. For that entire month, do not make any type of charge to your credit cards. You will need to still pay them on time, including your mortgage loans.

Instead of charging dining out or purchases to a credit card, only use cash. At first, you may find this very limiting, but imagine if you actually had all the money available to you that you are currently paying towards your debt each month. What you may find is that it is not only affordable to live on cash only but it may be a better lifestyle with less stress.

Making good decisions about credit is difficult to do, for anyone. Yet, you can easily accomplish this by spending your time making good financial decisions overall. The process will allow you to walk away finding yourself in a financially sound situation rather than a financially poor situation.

Use these ten tips to help you through the process of cleaning up your credit debt, not just today but going into the future, too.

# It takes time

One of the hardest elements to come from the entire process of improving your credit report is that it takes time. Sometimes, it takes a long time.

Those who find errors on their credit report will have the ability to remove them which may or may not give you a boost in your credit score. This depends greatly on the type of mistake you have removed.

For example, if you remove problems with:

- Your name

- Your address

- Past employers

- Other personal information

Chances are good that you will not see any change in your credit score since these items do not have a direct link to it.

On the other hand, if you find mistakes and have them removed like those in the following list:

- Debts that are not your own that are removed

- Outdated debts that are negatively impacting your credit score

- Collection accounts or judgments removed

- Inquiries

- Late payments, missing payments

- Over the limit reports

Or similar types of items, you should see a rise in your credit report for doing so. The amount of increase is really unknown since these complex formulas are not made public knowledge. The key is that over the long term, such as in the next six months to a year, you will no longer fell effects by the negative mistakes and this will help to boost the ongoing credit score you have.

TIPS FOR INCREASING YOUR CREDIT SCORE QUICKLY

There is no one way to raise your credit score. It is a combined effort of everything you do over the course of your life having to do with credit. The key here is to make the best choices overall. It is difficult and time consuming at best, but ultimately it will give you the best results over all. Maintaining your credit report and credit score is perhaps the longest journey you will be on throughout your life. There is never a time when you can take a break.

Some things to do to ensure the highest credit score is in reach:

1. Get your credit report clean of any errors on it by reporting and disputing these with each of the three credit reporting agencies, TransUnion, Equifax and Experian.

2. Keep an eye on your credit report. At least one time a year pull each report, examine it for potential mistakes and keep it clean.

3. Don't make payments late. One of the worst things you can do is send in your payment late. This is an instant warning sign to potential lenders: he or she is struggling with debt; beware! Send your payment in at least a week prior to the due date to ensure punctuality.

4. Do not go over your credit limit, like late payments this is another instance of struggling to make payments.

5. Keep your debts low. Pay off as much of or all of your debt each month. This shows to lenders you are a good credit risk and that you deserve more credit available to you.

6. Stay on top of the changes credit bureaus make to credit reporting. Small changes can make a significant difference in the way credit reporting happens and therefore what your credit is.

7. Use credit when you need to, but keep yourself in check.

8. Don't request multiple lines of credit at one time. When shopping for the best rates on a credit card, insurance product, or home loan, do so using estimated credit scores rather than allowing several companies to pull your report.

9. Keep your personal information personal. This includes your Social Security Number, address and historical information about you. Report any risks of identity theft as soon as you see them.

10. Live within your CASH means. In other words, make sure that 90 percent or more of your purchases are made using cash. Get off the credit lifestyle and you may find that your credit score goes up and you have more money in your pocket each month.

It does take a long time to build a successful credit report, but the process itself is one that teaches you how to use money wisely. It does not matter what has brought you to this point today. The only thing that truly makes a difference is what happens tomorrow.

Clean up your credit report first. Then, maintain it and use credit wisely. You will then have more doors open to you each month and you will have credit available to you when you need it.

It takes time and a little bit of effort, but it certainly can be done. You just need to be diligent about your spending habits and then monitor your credit reports so you know where you stand at any particular time.

Credit is an important part of our society, so cherish your credit history and your credit score. Make it just as important to you as your good name and keep it clean and pristine. It can mean so much to your future and your future is just as important as the present.

You know what they say: The past is the past, the future is the future, but today is a gift – that's why they call it the present!

Good Luck!

# Thank you

I truly hope this helps you get on the path to perfect credit. Whether for a home purchase, small business loan, or anything else that helps you invest in your future.

For more content, tools, and freebies visit www.yourrealtorkarina.com

www.ingramcontent.com/pod-product-compliance
Lightning Source LLC
Chambersburg PA
CBHW070856220526
45466CB00005B/2015